A Good Trick

Written by Roderick
Illustrated by Alex Brychta

A rug,

a sheet,

5

a big box,

a little box,

9

Kipper!

Talk about the story

Spot the difference

Find the five differences in the two pictures.

Fun at the Beach

Written by Roderick Hunt
Illustrated by Alex Brychta

Dad and Mum.

Mum and Dad.

Kipper, Chip and Biff.

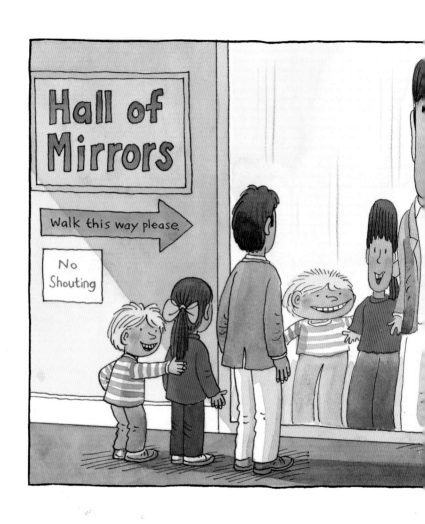

Kipper, Biff and Dad.

Mum, Chip and Floppy.

Chip, Biff and Kipper.

Dad and Floppy.

Oh Floppy!

Talk about the story

Spot the pair

Find the identical pair.